Stolen Focus
THE WORKBOOK

Copyright © 2023 by GuideGuru Publishing

All rights reserved. No part of this publication may be reproduced, distributed, or transmitted in any form or by any means, including photocopying, recording, or other electronic or mechanical methods, without the prior written permission of the publisher, except in the case of brief quotations embodied in critical reviews and certain other noncommercial uses permitted by copyright law. For permission requests, write to the publisher at the address below.

Disclaimer

The information in this workbook is intended for informational purposes only and is not intended to be a substitute for professional advice. The author is not a licensed professional, and the information in this workbook should not be taken as such. The author has tried their best to ensure that the information in this workbook is accurate and up-to-date, but cannot guarantee that it is error-free or complete. The author is still under development, and is always learning.

LESSONS IN THIS WORKBOOK:

Chapter 1: The Attention Crisis

Chapter 2: The Dopamine Trap

Chapter 3: The Mind-Wandering Myth

Chapter 4: The Attention Merchants

Chapter 5: The Path Forward

Chapter 1: The Attention Crisis

Lesson 1:

Assessing Your Attention

Attention Inventory: Reflect on your daily life and make a list of situations or activities where you tend to get easily distracted. Include both work-related and personal scenarios.

Distracted Consequences: Write about the consequences of distraction in your life. Consider how it affects your productivity, relationships, and overall well-being. Be specific about the negative outcomes you've experienced.

Identifying Distraction Triggers: List common triggers that lead to distraction for you. These could be notifications on your phone, multitasking habits, or specific stressors. Identify at least three triggers and describe how they impact your attention.

Lesson 2:

Minimizing Distractions

Digital Detox Plan: Create a plan for a digital detox where you intentionally disconnect from digital devices for a set period (e.g., a weekend). Write down the steps you'll take to implement this detox, including alternatives to digital activities.

Distraction-Free Workspace: If you work or study in a particular space, outline a plan to create a distraction-free environment. Identify potential distractions and describe how you'll eliminate or minimize them in that space.

Mindful Task Focus: Choose a task or activity that requires your full attention (e.g., reading a book or cooking a meal). Describe how you'll practice mindfulness by fully immersing yourself in the task, minimizing distractions, and being present.

Lesson 3:

Addressing Root Causes

Stress Management Plan: Develop a stress management plan that includes at least three strategies to reduce stress in your life. Write about how these strategies can help alleviate one of the root causes of distraction.

Tech Boundaries: Establish clear boundaries for your technology use. Describe how you'll limit screen time, especially during critical periods when you need to focus. Specify guidelines for checking emails, social media, and notifications.

Environmental Awareness: Identify sources of environmental pollution or distractions in your surroundings. Write down a plan to address or minimize these factors, whether it's noise pollution, clutter, or other disruptors.

Chapter 2: The Dopamine Trap

Lesson 1:

Understanding Dopamine and Its Impact

Dopamine in Daily Life: Reflect on your daily routine and activities that typically provide you with a sense of pleasure or reward. Write down at least three examples and describe the feelings associated with them.

Dopamine-Driven Technology Use: Identify specific technology-related habits or apps that you believe trigger the release of dopamine in your brain. Write about how often you engage in these habits and the impact they have on your attention and productivity.

Recognizing the Hook: Think about a recent instance when you felt compelled to check your phone or engage with social media. Describe the trigger that led to this behavior and the immediate gratification you experienced. Reflect on how this relates to the dopamine loop.

Lesson 2:

Breaking the Dopamine Loop

Digital Detox Plan: Create a plan for a digital detox where you intentionally reduce your screen time and exposure to dopamine-triggering technology. Write down the steps you'll take, such as setting boundaries or designating tech-free times.

Alternative Reward Activities: List at least three alternative activities that can provide a sense of pleasure and reward without relying on technology. Describe how you plan to incorporate these activities into your daily routine.

Mindful Technology Use: Develop a strategy for more mindful and intentional technology use. Write about specific practices you'll implement, such as turning off non-essential notifications or setting time limits on certain apps.

Lesson 3:

Cultivating Focus and Prioritization

Task Prioritization: List three important tasks or goals that often get pushed aside due to technology distractions. Describe how you'll prioritize these tasks and allocate focused time to work on them.

Focused Work Environment: Create a plan to establish a focused work or study environment. Describe the physical changes you'll make, such as decluttering your workspace or using noise-cancelling headphones, to minimize distractions.

Task Completion Reflection: Choose one of the tasks you prioritized in Activity 3. After completing it, reflect on how it felt to stay focused and accomplish the task without interruptions from technology. Write about the sense of satisfaction and accomplishment you experienced.

Chapter 3: The Mind-Wandering Myth

Lesson 1:

Embracing Mind-Wandering

Mind-Wandering Journal: Start a "Mind-Wandering Journal" to track instances when your mind naturally drifts away from focused tasks. Describe what you were doing, where your mind went, and any interesting thoughts or ideas that arose during these moments.

Mindful Mind-Wandering: Set aside a specific time each day for mindful mind-wandering. Find a quiet place, close your eyes, and allow your thoughts to wander freely. Afterward, write about the insights or creative ideas that emerged during this practice.

Mind-Wandering Opportunities: Identify situations or activities in your daily life where mind-wandering can be beneficial. These could include activities like taking a walk, showering, or commuting. Describe how you can protect and leverage these moments for creative thinking.

Lesson 2:

Technology and Mind-Wandering

Tech-Free Mind-Wandering: Plan a tech-free period in your day or week specifically dedicated to mind-wandering. Write down the duration and timing of this period and what activities you'll engage in to encourage mind-wandering.

Digital Detox Reflection: After a tech-free period, reflect on how it felt to disconnect from technology and allow your mind to wander freely. Write about any creative thoughts or solutions that emerged during this time.

Tech Use Awareness: Create a list of the technology devices or apps that most frequently disrupt your mind-wandering. Write down your intentions to limit or manage your use of these technologies to protect your cognitive freedom.

Lesson 3:

Cultivating Creativity

Creativity Spark: Choose a topic or challenge you're currently facing in your life or work. Spend time mind-wandering about this topic without any specific goals or constraints. Afterward, write down any creative insights or solutions that emerged.

Mind-Wandering Toolkit: Develop a "Mind-Wandering Toolkit" with resources or prompts that can help stimulate creative thinking. Include items like books, art supplies, or outdoor settings that inspire your mind to wander.

Mindful Problem Solving: The next time you encounter a problem or decision that requires creative thinking, approach it with mindful mind-wandering. Write about the process of allowing your mind to explore different perspectives and generate potential solutions.

Chapter 4: The Attention Merchants

Lesson 1:

Assessing Attention Merchants' Influence

Attention-Grabbing Apps: List the apps or digital platforms you use most frequently on your devices. Reflect on how these apps capture your attention and encourage prolonged use. Describe any tactics they employ to keep you engaged.

Advertising Impact: Think about the last time you made a purchase influenced by online advertising. Write about the product or service, the advertisement's content, and how it persuaded you to make the purchase. Reflect on whether the purchase was genuinely satisfying.

Data Privacy Review: Examine your digital privacy settings and permissions for apps and websites. Write about the extent to which you've allowed these platforms to collect data about you. Consider whether you're comfortable with the level of data sharing.

Lesson 2:

Protecting Your Attention

Notification Management: Develop a notification management strategy for your devices. Describe how you plan to customize and limit notifications to minimize interruptions and maintain your focus.

Tech-Free Zones: Identify specific areas or times in your daily life where you'll establish tech-free zones. Write about these zones, why they are important, and how they can help protect your attention and well-being.

Digital Detox Challenge: Set a digital detox challenge for yourself. Choose a day or weekend where you'll significantly reduce your screen time and digital interactions. Describe your motivations, goals, and activities you'll engage in during the detox.

Lesson 3:

Consumer Awareness and Advocacy

Advertising Analysis: Select an advertisement or sponsored content you encounter in your daily life, such as on social media or while browsing the web. Analyze the advertisement's persuasive techniques and its intent. Write about how you perceive the ad's impact on others.

Consumer Choices: Reflect on the products or services you consume regularly and consider the companies behind them. Write about whether you align with these companies' values and practices, and whether you're willing to make different choices based on this awareness.

Advocacy Plan: Develop a plan for advocating for responsible and ethical attention practices. Write about actions you can take, such as supporting privacy regulations, promoting digital literacy, or educating others about attention manipulation.

Chapter 5: The Path Forward

Lesson 1:

Mindful Technology Use

Digital Time Audit: Conduct a week-long audit of your digital screen time. Track the time you spend on various devices and apps. Write down the results and identify areas where you can reduce screen time.

Tech-Free Periods: Create a plan for incorporating tech-free periods into your daily or weekly routine. Describe when and how you'll disconnect from technology, including specific activities you'll engage in during these breaks.

Notification Reflection: Reflect on the impact of notifications on your attention. Write about how you plan to customize your notification settings to reduce distractions and interruptions.

Lesson 2:

Mind-Wandering and Brain Rest

Mind-Wandering Ritual: Establish a daily or weekly ritual for intentional mind-wandering. Describe the setting, duration, and practices you'll use to encourage your mind to wander freely and creatively.

Brain Rest Activities: List at least three activities that provide mental rest and recharge for you. These could include activities like meditation, reading fiction, or spending time in nature. Describe how you'll incorporate these activities into your schedule.

Reflection on Rest: After engaging in a brain-rest activity, reflect on how it made you feel and whether you noticed any positive effects on your mental clarity and creativity. Write about the value of these activities in your life.

Lesson 3:

Advocacy and Policy Support

Attention Protection Advocacy: Research policies and organizations dedicated to protecting individuals' attention and privacy. Write a plan for how you can support these efforts, whether through advocacy, donations, or spreading awareness.

Community Awareness: Consider organizing a community event or discussion on the topic of attention and technology use. Describe your plans for raising awareness and educating others about the importance of mindful attention.

Policy Engagement: Identify a specific policy or regulation related to technology and attention that you believe should be supported or amended. Write a letter or email to your local representative expressing your views and advocating for attention protection.

Made in the USA
Coppell, TX
18 May 2025